Charlie Cardigan in Putty (121) pattern on page 32

From left to right: Charlie Cardigan in Claret (104) and Charlie Cardigan in Moss (103) pattern on page 32, Catrin Jacket in Plum (162) and Claret (104) pattern on page 26, Birgitta Scarf in Plum (162) pattern on page 46, Stefan Jacket in Claret (104) and Fawn (160) pattern on page 40, and Emma Boatneck Jumper in Plum (162) and Fawn (160) pattern on page 58

CONTENTS

Stefan Jacket in Claret (104) and
Fawn (160) pattern on page 40

From left to right: Emma Boatneck Jumper in Midnight (101) and Fawn (160) and Emma Boatneck Jumper in Plum (162) and Fawn (160), pattern on page 58

Charlie Cardigan in Claret (104)
pattern on page 32

From left to right: Catrin Jacket in Putty (121) and Storm (102) pattern on page 26, Birgitta Cowl and Wristwarmers in Putty (121) patterns on page 46 and 54, and Charlie Cardigan in Putty (121) pattern on page 32

From left to right; Catrin Jacket in Plum (162) and Claret (104) pattern on page 26 and Stefan Jacket in Claret (104) and Fawn (160) pattern on page 40

Charlie Cardigan in Claret (104) and in Moss (103) pattern on page 32

From left to right: Charlie Cardigan in Putty (121) pattern on page 32, Catrin Jacket in Putty (121) and Storm (102) pattern on page 26, and Birgitta Cowl and Wristwarmers in Putty (121) patterns on page 46 and 54

Emma Boatneck Jumper in Midnight (101) and Fawn (160) pattern on page 58

BEFORE YOU START

Country Escape contains seven patterns in the MillaMia signature modern style, all made using our Naturally Soft Merino yarn. A warm, outdoorsy, beautiful lifestyle – something that we can all aspire to – is captured in these designs.

With an emphasis on muted, sophisticated colours we think the tight twist of our yarn is showcased to its best – demonstrating just how fabulous a hand knit can look when time and attention is lavished on it. So before you get started, please take the time to read the following basic information to help you make the most of your MillaMia pattern purchase.

TENSION / GAUGE

A standard tension is given for all the patterns in this book. As matching the tension affects the final shape and size of the item you are knitting, it can have a significant impact if it is not matched. Ensuring that you are knitting to the correct tension will result in the beautiful shape and lines of the original designs being achieved.

To check your tension we suggest that you knit a square according to the tension note at the start of each pattern (casting on an additional 10 or more stitches to the figure given in the tension note and knitting 5 to 10 more rows than specified in the tension note). You should knit the tension square in the stitch given in the note (e.g. stocking, garter, moss, etc). Once knitted, mark out a 10cm by 10cm / 4in by 4in square using pins and count the number of stitches and rows contained within. If your tension does not quite match the one given try switching to either finer needles (if you have too few stitches in your square) or thicker needles (if you have too many stitches) until you reach the desired tension.

YARN – SOME ADVICE

As there can be colour variations between dye lots when yarn is produced, we suggest that you buy all the yarn required for a project at the same time (with the same dye lot number) to ensure consistency of colour. The amount of yarn required for each pattern is based on average requirements meaning they are an approximate guide.

The designs in this book have been created specifically with a certain yarn composition in mind. The weight, quality, colours, comfort and finished knit effect of this yarn is ideally suited to these patterns. Substituting for another yarn may produce a garment that is different from the design and images in this book.

For some of the heavier items in our books we use a technique where we 'use the yarn double'. This simply means using two balls of yarn at once on a thicker needle (in our patterns a 5mm (US 8) needle) to produce a thicker, more structured quality to the knitted fabric.

SIZES

Alongside the patterns in this book we give actual measurements for the items – this should be used as a guide when choosing which size to knit.

Please note that where a chest measurement is given in the table at the top of each pattern this refers to the total measurement of the garment around the chest. When the cross chest measurement is given graphically in the accompanying diagrams this is half the around chest measurement.

SKILL LEVELS

Recognising that we are not all expert knitters we have graded each pattern in the book to allow you to gauge whether it is one that you feel confident to try.

USEFUL RESOURCES

We believe that using quality trims with our knitwear gives the garments a professional finishing touch. Visit your local yarn/ haberdashery shop for these items and MillaMia yarn or visit www.millamia.com to order yarn directly or find local stockists.

CARE OF YOUR GARMENT

See the ball band of MillaMia Naturally Soft Merino for washing and pressing instructions. Make sure you reshape your garments while they are wet after washing and dry flat.

LANGUAGE

This book has been written in UK English. However, where possible US terminology has also been included and we have provided a translation of the most common knitting terms that differ between US and UK knitting conventions on page 23. Remember that when a knitting pattern refers to the left and right sides of an item it is referring to the left or right side as worn, rather than as you are looking at it.

NEED SOME HELP?

We understand that sometimes even the most experienced knitter needs a bit of advice or help with a pattern, and of course beginners cannot be expected to know everything when they start out. If you need a starting point log on to our website www.millamia.com and search through the 'Making Knitting Easy' section.

In our books do not forget to look at the Hints and Tips section for each pattern. We are constantly updating these in reprints. Based on our experience of the customer queries we have had, we try to address concerns and questions upfront with these tips.

STILL STUCK?

We check every MillaMia pattern numerous times before we go to print and pride ourselves on having a good record to date with relatively few errata.

Despite this occasionally there can be errors in knitting patterns. If you see what you think is an error the best thing is to visit www.millamia.com where any errors that have been spotted will be published under 'Pattern Revisions'. If you cannot find the answer you are looking for, then do send an email (to info@millamia.com) or contact us via the website and we will get back to you.

Catrin Jacket in Plum (162) and Claret (104) pattern on page 26 and Birgitta Wristwarmers in Claret (104) pattern on page 54

ABBREVIATIONS

alt	alternate
approx	approximately
beg	begin(ning)
cont	continue
dec	decrease(ing)
foll	following
g-st	garter stitch
inc	increase(ing)
k or K	knit
k2 tog	knit two stitches together
m1	make one stitch by picking up the loop lying before the next stitch and knitting into back of it
m1pw	make one stitch by picking up the loop lying before the next stitch and purling into back of it
mths	months
p or P	purl
p2 tog	purl two stitches together
patt	pattern
psso	pass slipped stitch over
pwise	purlwise
rib2 tog	rib two stitches together according to rib pattern being followed
rem	remain(ing)
rep	repeat(ing)
skpo	slip one, knit one, pass slipped stitch over – one stitch decreased
sl	slip stitch
st(s)	stitch(es)
st st	stocking stitch
tbl	through back of loop
tog	together
yf	yarn forward
yo	yarn over
yon	yarn over needle to make a st
yrn	yarn round needle
y2rn	wrap the yarn two times around needle. On the following row work into each loop separately working tbl into second loop
[ ]	work instructions within brackets as many times as directed

---

UK AND US KNITTING TRANSLATIONS

UK	US
Cast off	Bind off
Colour	Color
Grey	Gray
Join	Sew
Moss stitch	Seed stitch
Tension	Gauge
Stocking stitch	Stockinette stitch
Yarn forward	Yarn over
Yarn over needle	Yarn over
Yarn round needle	Yarn over
y2rn	yo2

KNITTING NEEDLE CONVERSION CHART

Metric, mm	US size
2.75	2
3	2
3.25	3
4.5	7
5	8

From left to right: Charlie Cardigan in Claret (104) pattern on page 32, Birgitta Scarf in Plum (162) pattern on page 46, Charlie Cardigan in Moss (103) pattern on page 32, Emma Boatneck jumper in Plum (162) and Fawn (160) pattern on page 58, Cairn Jacket in Plum (162) and Claret (104) pattern on page 26, and Stefan Jacket in Claret (104) and Fawn (160) pattern on page 40.

CATRIN JACKET

SKILL LEVEL **Beginner / Improving**

SIZES / MEASUREMENTS

To fit bust

77-82	87-92	97-102	107-112	117-122	cm
30-32	34-36	38-40	42-44	46-48	in

ACTUAL MEASUREMENTS

Bust

89	100	111	122	133	cm
35	39 ½	43 ¾	48	52	in

Length to shoulder

60	62	64	66	68	cm
23 ½	24 ½	25 ¼	26	26 ¾	in

Sleeve length

44	44	45	45	46	cm
17 ½	17 ½	17 ¾	17 ¾	18	in

MATERIALS

16(21:24:28:30) 50g/1 ¾oz balls of MillaMia Naturally Soft Merino in Putty (121) (M).
2(2:2:3:3) balls in Storm (102) (C).
Pair each of 4.50mm (US 7) and 5mm (US 8) knitting needles.
10 large (approx 23mm/⅞in diameter) and 2 small (approx 18mm/¾in) buttons.

TENSION / GAUGE

18 sts and 26 rows to 10cm/4in square over st st using 5mm (US 8) needles and yarn double.

HINTS AND TIPS

The yarn used double results in a thick, warm structured garment with a great shape. If you are tall but thin bear in mind that you might need to add some extra length if knitting the smallest sizes.

NOTE

Use yarn double **throughout**.

ABBREVIATIONS

See page 23.

ALTERNATIVE COLOURWAYS

Plum	Claret	Fawn	Midnight	Storm	Putty
162	104	160	101	102	121

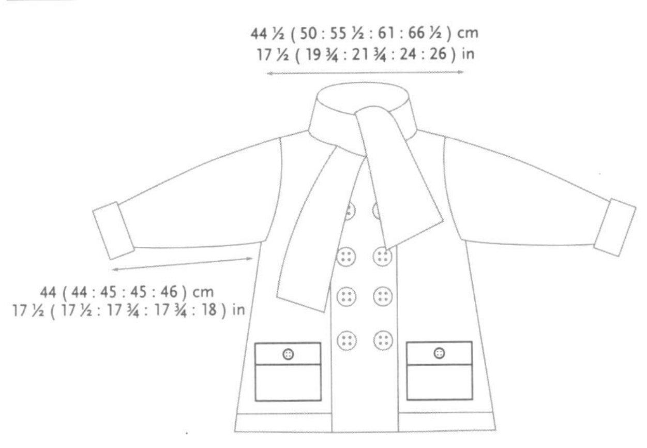

BACK

With 4.50mm (US 7) needles and M used double cast on 98(108:118:128:138) sts.
K 3 rows.
Change to C.
K 8 rows.
Change to 5mm (US 8) needles and M.
Beg with a k row cont in st st.
Work 8(10:10:12:12) rows.
Dec row K8, skpo, k to last 10 sts, k2 tog, k8.
Work 9 rows.
Rep the last 10 rows 6 times more, and then the dec row again. 82(92:102:112:122) sts.
Work straight until back measures 41(42:43:44:45)cm/16(16 ½:17:17 ½:17 ¾)in from cast on edge, ending with a p row.
Shape armholes
Cast off 6(7:8:9:10) sts at beg of next 2 rows. 70(78:86:94:102) sts.
Next row K2, skpo, k to last 4 sts, k2 tog, k2.
Next row P to end.
Rep the last 2 rows 5(6:7:8:9) times more. 58(64:70:76:82) sts.
Work straight until back measures 60(62:64:66:68)cm/23 ½(24 ½:25 ¼:26:26 ¾)in from cast on edge, ending with a p row.
Shape shoulders
Cast off 8(9:10:11:12) sts at beg of next 4 rows.
Cast off rem 26(28:30:32:34) sts.

LEFT FRONT

With 4.50mm (US 7) needles and M used double cast on 43(48:53:58:63) sts.
K 3 rows.
Change to C.
K 8 rows.
Change to 5mm (US 8) needles and M.
Beg with a k row cont in st st.
Work 8(10:10:12:12) rows.
Dec row K8, skpo, k to end.
Work 9 rows.
Rep the last 10 rows 6 times more, and then the dec row again. 35(40:45:50:55) sts.
Work straight until back measures 41(42:43:44:45)cm/16(16 ½:17:17 ½:17 ¾)in from cast on edge, ending with a p row.
Shape armhole
Next row Cast off 6(7:8:9:10) sts, k to end. 29(33:37:41:45) sts.
Next row P to end.
Next row K2, skpo, k to end.
Next row P to end.
Rep the last 2 rows 5(6:7:8:9) times more. 23(26:29:32:35) sts.
Work straight until 14(16:18:20:22) rows less have been worked than on back to shoulder shaping.
Shape neck
Next row K to last 4 sts, k2 tog, k2.
Next row P to end.
Rep the last 2 rows 6(7:8:9:10) times more. 16(18:20:22:24) sts.
Shape shoulder
Next row Cast off 8(9:10:11:12) sts at beg of next row.
Work 1 row.
Cast off rem 8(9:10:11:12) sts.

RIGHT FRONT

With 4.50mm (US 7) needles and M used double cast on 43(48:53:58:63) sts.
K 3 rows.
Change to C.
K 8 rows.
Change to 5mm (US 8) needles and M.
Beg with a k row cont in st st.

Work 8(10:10:12:12) rows.
Dec row K to last 10 sts, k2 tog, k8.
Work 9 rows.
Rep the last 10 rows 6 times more, and then the dec row again. 35(40:45:50:55) sts.
Work straight until back measures 41(42:43:44:45)cm/16(16 ½:17:17 ½:17 ¾)in from cast on edge, ending with a k row.

Shape armhole

Next row Cast off 6(7:8:9:10) sts, p to end. 29(33:37:41:45) sts.
Next row K to last 4 sts, k2 tog, k2.
Next row P to end.
Rep the last 2 rows 5(6:7:8:9) times more. 23(26:29:32:35) sts.
Work straight until 14(16:18:20:22) rows less have been worked than on back to shoulder shaping.

Shape neck

Next row K2, skpo, k to end.
Next row P to end.
Rep the last 2 rows 6(7:8:9:10) times more. 16(18:20:22:24) sts.
Next row K to end.

Shape shoulder

Next row Cast off 8(9:10:11:12) sts at beg of next row.
Work 1 row.
Cast off rem 8(9:10:11:12) sts.

SLEEVES

With 4.50mm (US 7) needles and M used double cast on 34(40:46:52:58) sts.
K 3 rows.
Change to C.
K 8 rows.
Change to 5mm (US 8) needles and M.
Beg with a k row cont in st st.
Work 8 rows.
Inc row K3, m1, k to last 3 sts, m1, k3.
Work 7 rows.
Rep the last 8 rows 9 times more, and then the inc row again. 56(62:68:74:80) sts.
Cont straight until sleeve measures 44(44:45:45:46) cm/17 ½(17 ½:17 ¾:17 ¾:18)in from cast on edge, ending with a p row.

Shape sleeve top

Cast off 6(7:8:9:10) sts at beg of next 2 rows. 44(48:52:56:60) sts.
Next row K to end.
Next row P to end.
Next row K2, skpo, k to last 4 sts, k2 tog, k2.
Next row P to end.
Rep the last 4 rows 7 times more. 28(32:36:40:44) sts.
Next row K2, skpo, k to last 4 sts, k2 tog, k2.
Next row P to end.
Rep the last 2 rows 1(2:3:4:5) times more. 24(26:28:30:32) sts.
Cast off 3 sts at beg of next 2 rows. 18(20:22:24:26) sts.
Cast off.

BUTTONBAND

With right side facing, starting at beg of neck shaping, using 4.50mm (US 7) needles and M used double, pick up and k102(106:110:114:118) sts evenly down left front edge.
1st rib row P2, [k2, p2] to end.
2nd rib row K2, [p2, k2] to end.
Rep the last 2 rows 11 times more, and then the first row again.
Cast off in rib.

BUTTONHOLE BAND

With right side facing, ending at beg of neck shaping, using 4.50mm (US 7) needles and M used double, pick up and k102(106:110:114:118) sts evenly up right front edge.
1st rib row P2, [k2, p2] to end.
2nd rib row K2, [p2, k2] to end.
3rd row As 1st row.
Buttonhole row Rib 40(44:48:52:56), [k2 tog, yrn, rib 12] 4 times, k2 tog, yrn, p2, k2.
Rib 17 rows.
Buttonhole row Rib 40(44:48:52:56), [k2 tog, yrn, rib 12] 4 times, k2 tog, yrn, p2, k2.
Rib 3 rows.
Cast off in rib.

POCKETS (make 2)

With 4.50mm (US 7) needles and M used double, cast on 23(24:25:26:27) sts.
K 1 row.
Change to C.
K 4 rows.
Change to 5mm (US 8) needles and M.
1st row K to end.
2nd row K1, p to last st, k1.
Rep the last 2 rows until pocket measures 16(17:17:18:18)cm/6 ¼(6 ¾:6 ¾:7:7)in from cast on edge, ending with a 1st row.
Next row K to end.
Next row K2, p to last 2 sts, k2.
Rep the last 2 rows twice more.
Change to C.
K 2 rows.
Change to M.
K 1 row.
Cast off.

NECK EDGING

Join shoulder seams.
With right side facing, starting and ending at beg of neck shaping, using 4.50mm (US 7) needles and M used double, pick up and k15(16:17:19:20) sts up right side of front neck, 26(28:30:32:34) sts from back neck, pick up and k15(16:17:19:20) sts down left side of front neck. 56(60:64:70:74) sts.
P 1 row.
Cast off.

SCARF

With 4.50mm (US 7) needles and M used double cast on 22(22:22:26:26) sts.
1st rib row K2, [p2, k2] to end.
2nd rib row P2, [k2, p2] to end.
These 2 rows form the rib.
Work 2 rows C, then continue in M until scarf measures 110(120:130:140:150)cm/43 ¼(47 ¼:51 ¼:55 ¼:59)in from cast on edge.
Work 2 rows C, then 2 rows M.
Cast off in M.

TO MAKE UP

Join side and sleeve seams. Sew in sleeves. Sew on buttons.
Fold scarf so that one 'half' is 10cm/4in longer than other half, with fold to centre of back neck and longer half on right side, sew scarf to neck edge edging.
Fold pocket tops to right side and secure with a button sewn centrally. Sew pockets in place.

CHARLIE CARDIGAN

SKILL LEVEL **Improving**

SIZES / MEASUREMENTS

To fit bust

82-87	92-97	102-107	112-117	cm
32-34	36-38	40-42	44-46	in

ACTUAL MEASUREMENTS

Bust

90	100	112	123	cm
35 ½	39 ½	44	48 ½	in

Length to shoulder

62	63	64	65	cm
24 ½	25	25 ¼	25 ½	in

Sleeve length

45cm/17 ¾in for all sizes

MATERIALS

14(15:16:17) 50g/1 ¾oz balls of MillaMia Naturally Soft Merino in Putty (121).

Pair each of 2.75mm (US 2) and 3.25mm (US 3) knitting needles.

Cable needle.

One large (approx 18mm/¾in diameter) and one small (approx 15mm/½in) diameter button.

45 (50 : 56 : 61 ½) cm
17 ¾ (19 ¾ : 22 : 24 ¼) in

45 cm
17 ¾ in

62 (63 : 64 : 65) cm
24 ½ (25 : 25 ¼ : 25 ½) in

110 cm / 43 ¼ in

TENSION / GAUGE

25 sts and 34 rows to 10cm/4in square over st st using 3.25mm (US 3) needles.

HINTS AND TIPS

Take care when placing the pockets using mattress stitch if possible. We actually think the pockets look best when placed near the bottom edges of the front pieces, on top of the garter stitch hem. See Moss and Claret items in the photos on the following pages.

ABBREVIATIONS

C6B, cable 6 back - slip next 3 sts onto cable needle and hold at back of work, k3, then k3 from cable needle.

C6F, cable 6 front - slip next 3 sts onto cable needle and hold at front of work, k3, then k3 from cable needle.

See also page 23.

ALTERNATIVE COLOURWAYS

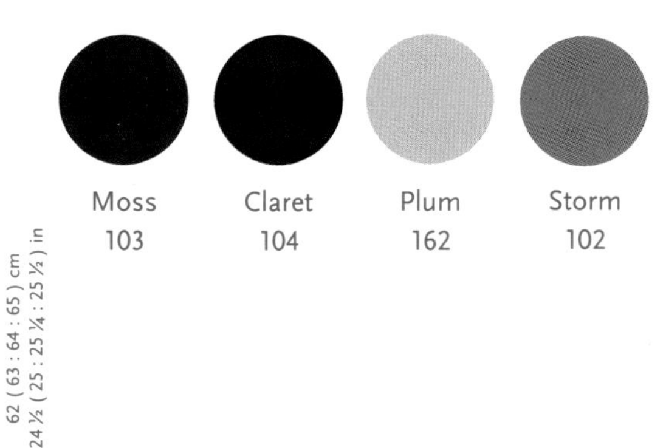

CABLE PANEL (worked over 19 sts)

1st row P2, k15, p2.
2nd and every foll wrong side row K2, p15, k2.
3rd row P2, k3, [C6F] twice, p2.
5th and 7th rows As 1st row.
9th row P2, [C6B] twice, k3, p2.
11th row As 1st row.
12th row As 2nd row.
These 12 rows form the cable panel and are repeated throughout.

BACK

With 2.75mm (US 2) needles cast on 130(144:158:172) sts.
K 13 rows.
Change to 3.25mm (US 3) needles.
Next row K30(34:38:42), p2, k3, [m1, k3] 3 times, p2, k38(44:50:56), p2, k3, [m1, k3] 3 times, p2, k30(34:38:42). 136(150:164:178) sts.
Next row P30(34:38:42), k2, p15, k2, p38(44:50:56), k2, p15, k2, p30(34:38:42).
Work in patt as follows:
Next row K30(34:38:42), work across the 3rd row of patt panel, k38(44:50:56), work across the 3rd row of patt panel, k30(34:38:42).
Next row P30(34:38:42), work across the 4th row of patt panel, p38(44:50:56), work across the 4th row of patt panel, p30(34:38:42).
These 2 rows set the 12 row cable patt.
Beg with 5th row of patt panel work a further 6 rows.
Dec row K10(12:14:16), skpo, patt to last 12(14:16:18) sts, k2 tog, k10(12:14:16).
Work a further 17 rows.
Rep the last 18 rows 5 times more, and then the dec row again. 122(136:150:164) sts.
Work straight until back measures 41cm/16 ¼in from cast on edge, ending with a wrong side row.

Shape armholes
Cast off 7(8:9:10) sts at beg of next 2 rows. 108(120:132:144) sts.
Next row K2, skpo, patt to last 4 sts, k2 tog, k2.
Next row Patt to end.
Rep the last 2 rows 6(8:10:12) times more. 94(102:110:118) sts.
Cont in patt until back measures 62(63:64:65)cm /24 ½(25:25 ¼:25 ½)in from cast on edge, ending with a wrong side row.
Shape shoulders
Cast off 10(11:12:13) sts at beg of next 4 rows and 9 sts at beg of foll 2 rows.
Leave rem 36(40:44:48) sts on a holder.

LEFT FRONT

With 2.75mm (US 2) needles cast on 69(76:83:90) sts.
K 13 rows.
Change to 3.25mm (US 3) needles.
Next row K30(34:38:42), p2, k3, [m1, k3] 3 times, p2, k23(26:29:32). 72(79:86:93) sts.
Next row K10, p13(16:19:22), k2, p15, k2, p30(34:38:42).
Work in patt as follows:
Next row K30(34:38:42), work across the 3rd row of patt panel, k23(26:29:32).
Next row K10, p13(16:19:22), work across the 4th row of patt panel, p30(34:38:42).
These 2 rows set the 12 row cable patt and g-st front border.
Beg with 5th row of patt panel work a further 6 rows.
Dec row K10(12:14:16), skpo, patt to end.
Work a further 17 rows.
Rep the last 18 rows 5 times more, and then the dec row again.
65(72:79:86) sts.

Work straight until front measures 41cm/16 ¼in from cast on edge, ending with a wrong side row.

Shape armhole

Next row Cast off 7(8:9:10) sts, patt to end. 58(64:70:76) sts.

Next row Patt to end.

Next row K2, skpo, patt to end.

Next row Patt to end.

Rep the last 2 rows 6(8:10:12) times more. 51(55:59:63) sts.

Cont in patt until front measures 54(55:55:56) cm /21 ¼(21 ¾:21 ¾:22)in from cast on edge, ending with a wrong side row.

Shape front neck

Next row Patt to last 15(16:17:18) sts, turn and leave these sts on a holder. 36(39:42:45) sts.

Dec one st at neck edge on next 7(8:9:10) rows. 29(31:33:35) sts.

Work straight until front measures the same as back to shoulder, ending at armhole edge.

Shape shoulder

Cast off 10(11:12:13) sts at beg of next and foll right side row.

Work 1 row.

Cast off rem 9 sts.

RIGHT FRONT

With 2.75mm (US 2) needles cast on 69(76:83:90) sts.

K 13 rows.

Change to 3.25mm (US 3) needles.

Next row K23(26:29:32), p2, k3, [m1, k3] 3 times, p2, k30(34:38:42). 72(79:86:93) sts.

Next row P30(34:38:42), k2, p15, k2, p13(16:19:22), k10.

Work in patt as follows:

Next row K23(26:29:32), work across the 3rd row of patt panel, k30(34:38:42).

Next row P30(34:38:42), work across the 4th row of patt panel, p13(16:19:22), k10.

These 2 rows set the 12 row cable patt and g-st front border.

Beg with 5th row of patt panel work a further 6 rows.

Dec row Patt to last 12(14:16:18) sts, k2 tog, k10(12:14:16).

Work a further 17 rows.

Rep the last 18 rows 5 times more, and then the dec row again.

65(72:79:86) sts.

Work straight until front measures 41cm/16 ¼in from cast on edge, ending with a right side row.

Shape armhole

Next row Cast off 7(8:9:10) sts, patt to end. 58(64:70:76) sts.

Next row Patt to last 4 sts, k2 tog, k2.

Next row Patt to end.

Rep the last 2 rows 6(8:10:12) times more. 51(55:59:63) sts.

Cont in patt until front measures 54(55:55:56)cm /21 ¼(21 ¾:21 ¾:22)in from cast on edge, ending with a wrong side row.

Shape front neck

Next row Patt 15(16:17:18) sts, leave these sts on a holder, patt to end.

36(39:42:45) sts.

Dec one st at neck edge on next 7(8:9:10) rows. 29(31:33:35) sts.

Work straight until front measures the same as back to shoulder, ending at armhole edge.

Shape shoulder

Cast off 10(11:12:13) sts at beg of next and foll wrong side row.

Work 1 row.

Cast off rem 9 sts.

SLEEVES

With 2.75mm (US 2) needles cast on 59(69:69:79) sts.

1st row (right side) P3, [k3, p2] to last 6 sts, k3, p3.

2nd row K3, [p3, k2] to last 6 sts, p3, k3.

Rep the last 2 rows 5 times more, and then the first row again.

Inc row (wrong side) Rib 26(31:31:36), m1, rib 7, m1, rib 26(31:31:36). 61(71:71:81) sts.

Change to 3.25mm (US 3) needles.

Work in patt as follows:

1st row K21(26:26:31), work across 3rd row of patt panel, k21(26:26:31).

2nd row P21(26:26:31), work across 4th row of patt panel, p21(26:26:31).

These 2 rows set the cable panel.

Beg with 5th row of patt panel work a further 8(10:10:12) rows.

Inc row K3, m1, patt to last 3 sts, m1, k3.

Work 9(9:7:7) rows.

Rep the last 10(10:8:8) rows 11(10:13:12) times more, and then the inc row again.

87(95:101:109) sts.

Cont straight until sleeve measures 45cm/17 ¾in from cast on edge, ending with a wrong side row.

Shape sleeve top

Cast off 7(8:9:10) sts at beg of next 2 rows.

73(79:83:89) sts.

Next row K2, skpo, patt to last 4 sts, k2 tog, k2.

Next row Patt to end.

Rep the last 2 rows 21(22:23:24) times more.

29(33:35:39) sts.

Cast off 2 sts at beg of next 6 rows. 17(21:23:27) sts.

Cast off.

NECKBAND

Join shoulder seams.

With right side facing and 2.75mm (US 2) needles slip 15(16:17:18) sts from right front neck holder onto a needle, join in yarn, pick up and k23 sts up right front neck, k36(40:44:48) sts from back neck holder, pick up and k23 sts down left front neck, k15(16:17:18) from left front holder. 112(118:124:130) sts.

Cont in g-st.

Cast on 4 sts at beg of next 2 rows.

120(126:132:138) sts.

K 3 rows.

Next row (buttonhole row) K2, k2 tog, y2rn, skpo, k to last 4 sts, k2 tog, yf, k2.

K 5 rows.

Cast off.

POCKETS (make 2)

With 3.25mm (US 3) needles cast on 36 sts.
1st row (right side) K10, p2, k12, p2, k10.
2nd row P10, k2, p12, k2, p10.
3rd row K10, p2, k3, [m1, k3] 3 times, p2, k10. 39 sts.
4th row P10, k2, p15, k2, p10.
Work in patt as follows:
Next row K10, work across the 3rd row of patt panel, k10.
Next row P10, work across the 4th row of patt panel, p10.
These 2 rows set the 12 row cable patt.
Beg with 5th row of patt panel work a further 33 rows.
Next row P10, k2, [p2 tog, p1] 5 times, k2, p10. 34 sts.
Change to 2.75mm (US 2) needles.
K 10 rows.
Cast off.

BELT

Using 2.75mm (US 2) needles, cast on 10 sts.
Cont in g-st until belt measures 110cm/43 ¼in.
Cast off.

BELT CARRIERS (make 2)

Using 2.75mm (US 2) needles, cast on 12 sts.
K 1 row.
Cast off.

MAKE UP

Join side and sleeve seams. Sew in sleeves. Sew on pockets. Sew belt carriers to side seam. Sew on buttons to correspond with buttonholes. The larger button on right side of left front neckband, the smaller button on wrong side of right front neckband.

STEFAN JACKET

SKILL LEVEL **Beginner / Improving**

SIZES / MEASUREMENTS

To fit chest

92-97	102-107	112-117	122-127	cm
36-38	40-42	44-46	48-50	in

ACTUAL MEASUREMENTS

Chest

100	112	124	134	cm
39	44	49	53	in

Length to shoulder

65	67	69	71	cm
25 ½	26 ½	27 ¼	28	in

Sleeve length

50cm/19 ¾in for all sizes

MATERIALS

14(16:18:20) 50g/1 ¾oz balls of MillaMia Naturally Soft Merino in Claret (104) (M).
One ball of Fawn (160) (C).
Pair each of 3mm (US 2) and 3.25mm (US 3) knitting needles.
Seven buttons approx 18mm/¾in diameter.

TENSION / GAUGE

25 sts and 34 rows to 10cm/4in square over st st using 3.25mm (US 3) needles.

HINTS AND TIPS

Take care when placing the arm and shoulder patches – for a quality finish we suggest using mattress stitch. If you do not constantly want to be undoing the buttons this jacket can be left almost all buttoned up and used as a jumper too.

ABBREVIATIONS

See page 23.

ALTERNATIVE COLOURWAYS

Storm 102 Putty 121

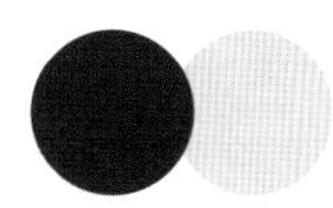

Midnight 101 Fawn 160

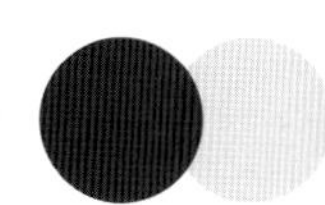

Moss 103 Fawn 160

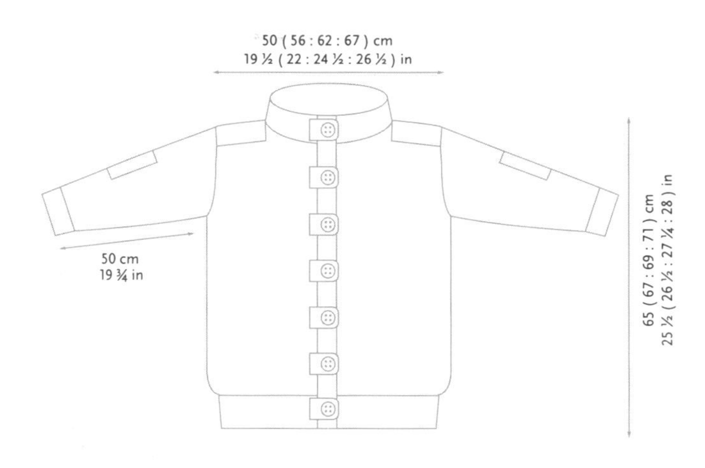

BACK

With 3mm (US 2) needles and M cast on 128(142:156:170) sts.

1st row K3, [p3, k4] to last 6 sts, p3, k3.

2nd row P to end.

Rep the last 2 rows 9 times more.

Change to 3.25mm (US 3) needles.

Beg with a k row, work in st st until back measures 43(44:45:46)cm/17(17 ¼:17 ¾:18)in from cast on edge, ending with a p row.

Shape armholes

Cast off 8(9:10:11) sts at beg of next 2 rows. 112(124:136:148) sts.

Next row K2, skpo, k to last 4 sts, k2 tog, k2.

Next row P to end.

Rep the last 2 rows 7(8:9:10) times more. 96(106:116:126) sts.

Cont straight until back measures 65(67:69:71)cm/25 ½(26 ½:27 ¼:28)in.

Shape shoulders

Cast off 9(10:11:12) sts at beg of next 6 rows.

Leave rem 42(46:50:54) sts on a holder.

RIGHT FRONT

With 3mm (US 2) needles and M cast on 72(79:86:93) sts.

1st row P1, [k2, p1] 4 times, [k4, p3] 8(9:10:11) times, k3.

2nd row P to end.

Rep the last 2 rows 9 times more.

Change to 3.25mm (US 3) needles.

Next row (right side) P1, [k2, p1] 4 times, k59(66:73:80).

Next row P to end.

These 2 rows form the st st with rib border.

Work straight until front measures 43(44:45:46)cm/17(17 ¼:17 ¾:18)in from cast on edge, ending with a right side row.

Shape armhole

Cast off 8(9:10:11) sts at beg of next row. 64(70:76:82) sts.

Next row Patt to last 4 sts, k2 tog, k2.

Next row Patt to end.

Rep the last 2 rows 7(8:9:10) times more. 56(61:66:71) sts.

Work straight until front measures 55(56:56:57) cm /21 ½(22:22:22 ½)in from cast on edge, ending with a wrong side row.

Shape neck

Next row Patt 18(19:20:21) sts, leave these sts on a holder, k to end.

Next row P to end.

Next row K2, skpo, k to end.

Rep the last 2 rows until 27(30:33:36) sts rem.

Cont straight until front measures same as back to shoulder, ending at armhole edge.

Shape shoulder

Cast off 9(10:11:12) sts at beg of next and foll wrong side row.

Work 1 row.

Cast off rem 9(10:11:12) sts.

Mark positions for 6 buttons, the first 2.5cm/1in from cast on edge, the sixth 3cm/1 ¼in from neck edge and the rem 4 spaced evenly between.

LEFT FRONT

Throughout left front work buttonholes to match markers on right front as folls:

Buttonhole row Patt to last 7 sts, k2 tog, y2rn, skpo, k2, p1.

With 3mm (US 2) needles and M cast on 72(79:86:93) sts.

1st row K3, [p3, k4] 8(9:10:11) times, p1, [k2, p1] 4 times.

2nd row P to end.

Rep the last 2 rows 9 times more.
Change to 3.25mm (US 3) needles.
Next row (right side) K59(66:73:80), p1, [k2, p1] 4 times.
Next row P to end.
These 2 rows form the st st with rib border.
Work straight until front measures 43(44:45:46)cm /17(17 ¼:17 ¾:18)in from cast on edge, ending with a wrong side row.

Shape armhole

Cast off 8(9:10:11) sts at beg of next row. 64(70:76:82) sts.
Next row Patt to end.
Next row K2, skpo, patt to end.
Next row Patt to end.
Rep the last 2 rows 7(8:9:10) times more. 56(61:66:71) sts.
Work straight until front measures 55(56:56:57)cm /21 ½(22:22:22 ½)in from cast on edge, ending with a wrong side row.

Shape neck

Next row Patt to last 18(19:20:21) sts, leave these sts on a holder.
Next row P to end.
Next row K to last 4 sts, k2 tog, k2.
Rep the last 2 rows until 27(30:33:36) sts rem.
Cont straight until front measures same as back to shoulder, ending at armhole edge.

Shape shoulder

Cast off 9(10:11:12) sts at beg of next and foll right side row.
Work 1 row.
Cast off rem 9(10:11:12) sts.

SLEEVES

With 3mm (US 2) needles and M cast on 65(72:79:86) sts.
1st row K3, [p3, k4] to last 6 sts, p3, k3.
2nd row P3, [k3, p4] to last 6 sts, k3, p3.
Rep the last 2 rows 9 times more.
Change to 3.25mm (US 3) needles.
Beg with a k row, work in st st.
Work 4 rows.
1st inc row K3, m1, k to last 3 sts, m1, k3.
Work 6 rows.
2nd inc row P3, m1pw, p to last 3 sts, m1pw, p3.
Work 6 rows.
Rep the last 14 rows 9 times more, and then the 1st inc row again.
107(114:121:128) sts.
Cont straight until sleeve measures 50cm/19 ¾in from cast on edge, ending with a p row.

Shape top

Cast off 8(9:10:11) sts at beg of next 2 rows. 91(96:101:106) sts.
Next row K2, skpo, k to last 4 sts, k2 tog, k2.
Next row P to end.
Rep the last 2 rows 7(8:9:10) times more. 75(78:81:84) sts.
Next row K2, skpo, k to last 4 sts, k2 tog, k2.
Next row P to end.
Next row K to end.
Next row P to end.
Rep the last 4 rows 3 times more. 67(70:73:76) sts.
Cast off 4 sts at beg of next 12 rows.
Cast off.

NECKBAND

Join shoulder seams.
With right side facing and 3mm (US 2) needles slip 18(19:20:21) sts from right front neck holder onto a needle, join in M, pick up and k23(26:26:29) sts up right front neck, k42(46:50:54) sts from back neck holder, pick up and k23(26:26:29) sts down left front neck, patt 18(19:20:21) from left front holder. 124(136:142:154) sts.
Next row P to end.
Next row P1, [k2, p1] to end.
These 2 rows form the rib.
Work a further 11 rows.
Buttonhole row Patt to last 7 sts, k2 tog, y2rn, skpo, k2, p1.
Work a further 13 rows.
Cast off in patt.

BUTTONHOLE TABS (make 7)

With 3mm (US 2) needles and M cast on 10 sts.
1st row P1, [k2, p1] 3 times.
2nd row P to end.
Rep the last 2 rows once more.
Next row (buttonhole row) P1, k2, p2 tog, y2rn, skpo, k2, p1.
Work a further 17 rows in patt.
Cast off in patt.

ELBOW PATCHES (make 2)

With 3mm (US 2) needles and C cast on 37 sts.
1st row P1, [k2, p1] 12 times.
2nd row P to end.
Rep the last 2 rows 24 times more.
Cast off in patt.

SHOULDER PATCHES (make 2)

With 3mm (US 2) needles and C cast on 46 sts.
1st row P1, [k2, p1] 15 times.
2nd row P to end.
Rep the last 2 rows 14 times more.
Cast off in patt.

TO MAKE UP

Join side and sleeve seams. Sew in sleeves. Sew on buttonhole tabs and buttons. Sew on shoulder and elbow patches.

BIRGITTA COWL & SCARF

SKILL LEVEL **Improving**

SIZES / MEASUREMENTS

Cowl

One size measuring 122cm/48in around

Scarf

One size measuring 150cm/59in long and approx 13cm/5in wide

MATERIALS

Cowl

Four 50g/1 ¾oz balls of MillaMia Naturally Soft Merino in Putty (121).

Pair of 3.25mm (US 3) knitting needles.

Cable needle.

Scarf

Four 50g/1 ¾oz balls of MillaMia Naturally Soft Merino in Plum (162).

Pair of 3.25mm (US 3) knitting needles.

Cable needle.

TENSION / GAUGE

27 sts and 38 rows to 10cm/4in square over Irish moss st using 3.25mm (US 3) needles.

HINTS AND TIPS

A beautiful cable and diamond pattern. Bear in mind that the pattern inside the diamond panel is an Irish moss stitch – not a regular moss stitch. Block well to keep flat once finished.

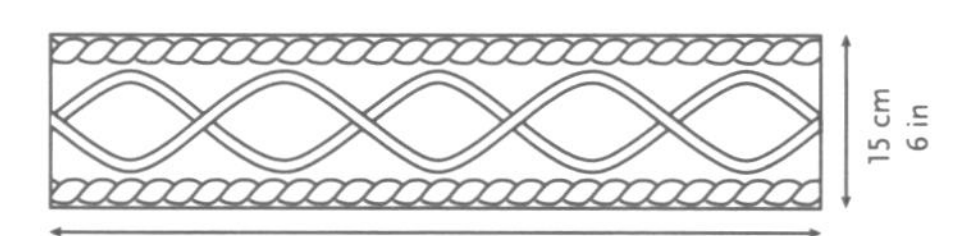

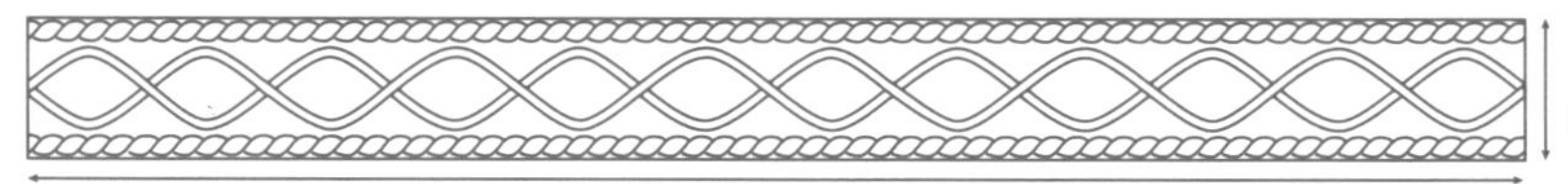

ABBREVIATIONS

T4R - slip next st onto cable needle and hold at back of work, k3, then p1 from cable needle.

T4L - slip next 3 sts onto cable needle and hold to front of work, p1, then k3 from cable needle.

C4R - slip next st onto cable needle and hold at back of work, k3, then k1 from cable needle.

C4L - slip next 3 sts onto cable needle and hold to front of work, k1, then k3 from cable needle.

C7B - slip next 4 sts onto cable needle and hold at back of work, k3, then k4 from cable needle.

C10F - slip next 5 sts on a cable needle and hold at front of work, k5 then k5 from cable needle.

C10B - slip next 5 sts on a cable needle and hold at back of work, k5 then k5 from cable needle.

C6F - slip next 3 sts on a cable needle and hold at front of work, k3 then k3 from cable needle.

C6B - slip next 3 sts on a cable needle and hold at back of work, k3 then k3 from cable needle.

See also page 23.

ALTERNATIVE COLOURWAYS

Snow 124	Fawn 160	Scarlet 140	Forget me not 120

DIAMOND PANEL (worked over 29 sts)

1st row (right side) P10, C4R, p1, C4L, p10.
2nd row K10, p4, k1, p4, k10.
3rd row P9, C4R, p1, k1, p1, C4L, p9.
4th row K9, p4, k1, p1, k1, p4, k9.
5th row P8, C4R, [p1, k1] twice, p1, C4L, p8.
6th row K8, p4, [k1, p1] twice, k1, p4, k8.
7th row P7, C4R, [p1, k1] 3 times, p1, C4L, p7.
8th row K7, p4, [k1, p1] 3 times, k1, p4, k7.
9th row P6, C4R, [p1, k1] 4 times, p1, C4L, p6.
10th row K6, p4, [k1, p1] 4 times, k1, p4, k6.
11th row P5, C4R, [p1, k1] 5 times, p1, C4L, p5.
12th row K5, p4, [k1, p1] 5 times, k1, p4, k5.
13th row P4, C4R, [p1, k1] 6 times, p1, C4L, p4.
14th row K4, p4, [k1, p1] 6 times, k1, p4, k4.
15th row P3, C4R, [p1, k1] 7 times, p1, C4L, p3.
16th row K3, p4, [k1, p1] 7 times, k1, p4, k3.
17th row P2, C4R, [p1, k1] 8 times, p1, C4L, p2.
18th row K2, p4, [k1, p1] 8 times, k1, p4, k2.
19th row P1, C4R, [p1, k1] 9 times, p1, C4L, p1.
20th row K1, p4, [k1, p1] 9 times, k1, p4, k1.
21st row C4R, [p1, k1] 10 times, p1, C4L.
22nd row P4, [k1, p1] 10 times, k1, p4.
23rd row K3, [p1, k1] 11 times, p1, k3.
24th row P3, [k1, p1] 11 times, k1, p3.
25th row T4L, [p1, k1] 10 times, p1, T4R.
26th row K1, p3, [k1, p1] 10 times, k1, p3, k1.
27th row P1, T4L, [p1, k1] 9 times, p1, T4R, p1.
28th row K2, p3, [k1, p1] 9 times, k1, p3, k2.
29th row P2, T4L, [p1, k1] 8 times, p1, T4R, p2.
30th row K3, p3, [k1, p1] 8 times, k1, p3, k3.
31st row P3, T4L, [p1, k1] 7 times, p1, T4R, p3.
32nd row K4, p3, [k1, p1] 7 times, k1, p3, k4.
33rd row P4, T4L, [p1, k1] 6 times, p1, T4R, p4.
34th row K5, p3, [k1, p1] 6 times, k1, p3, k5.
35th row P5, T4L, [p1, k1] 5 times, p1, T4R, p5.
36th row K6, p3, [k1, p1] 5 times, k1, p3, k6.
37th row P6, T4L, [p1, k1] 4 times, p1, T4R, p6.
38th row K7, p3, [k1, p1] 4 times, k1, p3, k7.
39th row P7, T4L, [p1, k1] 3 times, p1, T4R, p7.
40th row K8, p3, [k1, p1] 3 times, k1, p3, k8.
41st row P8, T4L, [p1, k1] twice, p1, T4R, p8.
42nd row K9, p3, [k1, p1] twice, k1, p3, k9.
43rd row P9, T4L, p1, k1, p1, T4R, p9.
44th row K10, p3, k1, p1, k1, p3, k10.
45th row P10, T4L, p1, T4R, p10.
46th row K11, p3, k1, p3, k11.
47th row P11, C7B, p11.
48th row K11, p7, k11.
These 48 rows **form** the Diamond Panel and are repeated.

TO MAKE COWL

With 3.25mm (US 3) needles cast on 55 sts.
1st Foundation row K1, p1, k11, work across 47th row of Diamond Panel, k11, p1, k1.
2nd Foundation row P1, k1, p11, work across 48th row of Diamond Panel, p11, k1, p1.
Work in patt.
1st row P1, k1, p1, k10, work across 1st row of Diamond Panel, k10, p1, k1, p1.
2nd row K1, p1, k1, p10, work across 2nd row of Diamond Panel, p10, k1, p1, k1.
3rd row K1, p1, k11, work across 3rd row of Diamond Panel, k11, p1, k1.
4th row P1, k1, p11, work across 4th row of Diamond Panel, p11, k1, p1.
5th row P1, k1, p1, k10, work across 5th row of Diamond Panel, k10, p1, k1, p1.
6th row K1, p1, k1, p10, work across 6th row of Diamond Panel, p10, k1, p1, k1.
7th row K1, p1, k1, C10F, work across 7th row of Diamond Panel, C10B, k1, p1, k1.
8th row P1, k1, p11, work across 8th row of Diamond Panel, p11, k1, p1.
9th row P1, k1, p1, k10, work across 9th row of Diamond Panel, k10, p1, k1, p1.
10th row K1, p1, k1, p10, work across 10th row of Diamond Panel, p10, k1, p1, k1.
11th row K1, p1, k11, work across 11th row of Diamond Panel, k11, p1, k1.
12th row P1, k1, p11, work across 12th row of Diamond Panel, p11, k1, p1.
These 12 rows **set** the position for the Diamond Panel and **form** the 12 row cable panel with moss st edges.
Cont in patt until 10 Diamond Panels have been worked, ending with a 47th diamond patt row.
Cast off in patt.
Join cast on edge to cast off edge.

TO MAKE SCARF

With 3.25mm (US 3) needles cast on 47 sts.
1st Foundation row K1, p1, k7, work across 47th row of Diamond Panel, k7, p1, k1.
2nd Foundation row P1, k1, p7, work across 48th row of Diamond Panel, p7, k1, p1.
Work in patt.
1st row P1, k1, p1, k6, work across 1st row of Diamond Panel, k6, p1, k1, p1.
2nd row K1, p1, k1, p6, work across 2nd row of Diamond Panel, p6, k1, p1, k1.
3rd row K1, p1, k1, C6F, work across 3rd row of Diamond Panel, C6B, k1, p1, k1.
4th row P1, k1, p7, work across 4th row of Diamond Panel, p7, k1, p1.
5th row P1, k1, p1, k6, work across 5th row of Diamond Panel, k6, p1, k1, p1.
6th row K1, p1, k1, p6, work across 6th row of Diamond Panel, p6, k1, p1, k1.
7th row K1, p1, k7, work across 7th row of Diamond Panel, k7, p1, k1.
8th row P1, k1, p7, work across 8th row of Diamond Panel, p7, k1, p1.
These 8 rows **set** the position for the Diamond Panel and **form** the 8 row cable panel with moss st edges.
Cont in patt until 12 Diamond Panels have been worked, ending with a 47th diamond patt row.
Cast off in patt.

BIRGITTA WRISTWARMERS

SKILL LEVEL **Improving**

SIZES / MEASUREMENTS

One size 22cm/ 8 ½in long by approx 8cm/3 ¼in wide

MATERIALS

Two 50g/1 ¾oz balls of MillaMia Naturally Soft Merino in Claret (104).
Pair of 3.25mm (US 3) knitting needles.
Cable needle.

TENSION / GAUGE

27 sts and 38 rows to 10cm/4in square over Irish moss st using 3.25mm (US 3) needles.

HINTS AND TIPS

A wonderful quick knit making an ideal gift. Pay attention in setting the cable pattern and then enjoy the process. Bear in mind that the pattern inside the diamond panel is an Irish moss stitch - not a regular moss stitch. Knit the matching cowl or scarf if you fall in love with the pattern.

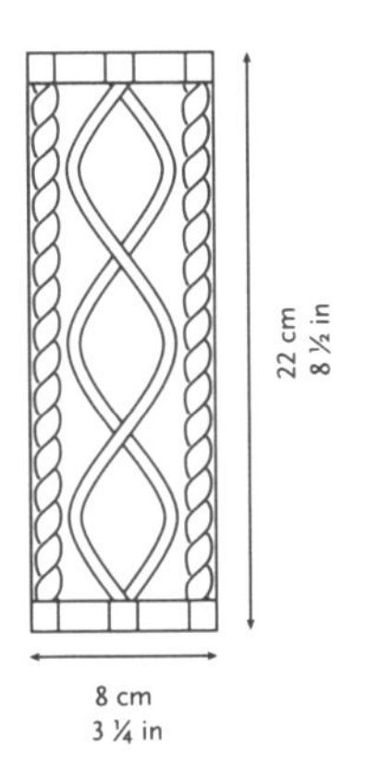

ABBREVIATIONS

T3R - slip next st onto cable needle and hold at back of work, k2, then p1 from cable needle.
T3L - slip next 2 sts onto cable needle and hold to front of work, p1, then k2 from cable needle.
C3R - slip next st onto cable needle and hold at back of work, k2, then k1 from cable needle.
C3L - slip next 2 sts onto cable needle and hold to front of work, k1, then k2 from cable needle.
C5B - slip next 3 sts onto cable needle and hold at back of work, k2, then k3 from cable needle.
C4F - slip next 2 sts on a cable needle and hold at front of work, k2 then k2 from cable needle.
C4B - slip next 2 sts on a cable needle and hold at back of work, k2 then k2 from cable needle.
See also page 23.

ALTERNATIVE COLOURWAYS

Fawn	Putty	Petal	Plum
160	121	122	162

DIAMOND PANEL (worked over 15 sts)

1st row (right side) P4, C3R, p1, C3L, p4.
2nd row K4, p3, k1, p3, k4.
3rd row P3, C3R, p1, k1, p1, C3L, p3.
4th row K3, p3, k1, p1, k1, p3, k3.
5th row P2, C3R, [p1, k1] twice, p1, C3L, p2.
6th row K2, p3, [k1, p1] twice, k1, p3, k2.
7th row P1, C3R, [p1, k1] 3 times, p1, C3L, p1.
8th row K1, p3, [k1, p1] 3 times, k1, p3, k1.
9th row C3R, [p1, k1] 4 times, p1, C3L.
10th row P3, [k1, p1] 4 times, k1, p3.
11th row K2, [p1, k1] 5 times, p1, k2.
12th row P2, [k1, p1] 5 times, k1, p2.
13th row T3L, [p1, k1] 4 times, p1, T3R.
14th row K1, p2, [k1, p1] 4 times, k1, p2, k1.
15th row P1, T3L, [p1, k1] 3 times, p1, T3R, p1.
16th row K2, p2, [k1, p1] 3 times, k1, p2, k2.
17th row P2, T3L, [p1, k1] twice, p1, T3R, p2.
18th row K3, p2, [k1, p1] twice, k1, p2, k3.
19th row P3, T3L, p1, k1, p1, T3R, p3.
20th row K4, p2, k1, p1, k1, p2, k4.
21st row P4, T3L, p1, T3R, p4.
22nd row K5, p5, k5.
23rd row P5, C5B, p5.
24th row K5, p5, k5.
These 24 rows form the Diamond Panel and are repeated.

TO MAKE (make 4 pieces alike)

With 3.25mm (US 3) needles cast on 25 sts.
1st row P2, k3, p5, k5, p5, k3, p2.
2nd row K2, p3, k5, p5, k5, p3, k2.
Rep the last 2 rows twice more.
Work in patt.
1st Foundation row P2, k3, work across 23rd row of Diamond Panel, k3, p2.
2nd Foundation row K2, p2, m1pw, p1, work across 24th row of Diamond Panel, p1, m1pw, p2, k2.
27 sts.
Work in patt.
1st row P2, C4F, work across 1st row of Diamond Panel, C4B, p2.
2nd row K2, p4, work across 2nd row of Diamond Panel, p4, k2.
3rd row P2, k4, work across 3rd row of Diamond Panel, k4, p2.
4th row K2, p4, work across 4th row of Diamond Panel, p4, k2.
These 4 rows **set** the position for the Diamond Panel and **form** the 4 st cable panels with reverse st st edges.
Cont in patt until 3 Diamond Panels have been worked, ending with a 23rd diamond patt row and working a p2 tog across each 4 st cable.
25 sts.
1st row K2, p3, k5, p5, k5, p3, k2.
2nd row P2, k3, p5, k5, p5, k3, p2.
Rep the last 2 rows twice more.
Cast off in rib.

MAKE UP

Join side seams leaving a gap for thumb.

EMMA BOATNECK JUMPER

SKILL LEVEL **Beginner**

SIZES / MEASUREMENTS

To fit bust

82	87	92	97	102	107	112	cm
32	34	36	38	40	42	44	in

ACTUAL MEASUREMENTS

Chest

82	89	95	102	108	114	121	cm
32	35	37 ½	40	42 ½	45	47 ½	in

Length to shoulder

60	60	61	61	62	62	63	cm
23 ¾	23 ¾	24	24	24 ½	24 ½	24 ¾	in

Sleeve length

33cm/ 13in for all sizes

MATERIALS

6(8:8:9:9:10:10) 50g/1 ¾oz balls of MillaMia Naturally Soft Merino in Midnight (101) (M).
5(6:6:7:7:8:8) balls in Fawn (160) (C).
Pair each of 3mm (US 2) and 3.25mm (US 3) knitting needles.
3mm (US 2) and 3.25mm (US 3) circular needles.

TENSION / GAUGE

25 sts and 34 rows to 10cm/4in square over st st using 3.25mm (US 3) needles.

HINTS AND TIPS

A simple stocking stitch jumper – great for the beginner knitter wanting to try a bit of shaping for the first time. Circular needles are used due to the number of stitches worked, working in rows – not in the round.

ABBREVIATIONS

See page 23.

ALTERNATIVE COLOURWAYS

Plum 162 Fawn 160

Scarlet 140 Fawn 160

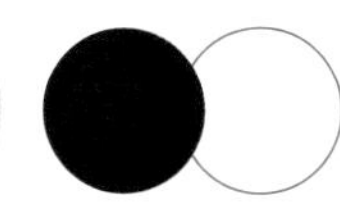

Midnight 101 Snow 124

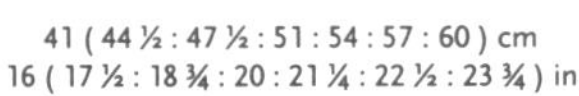

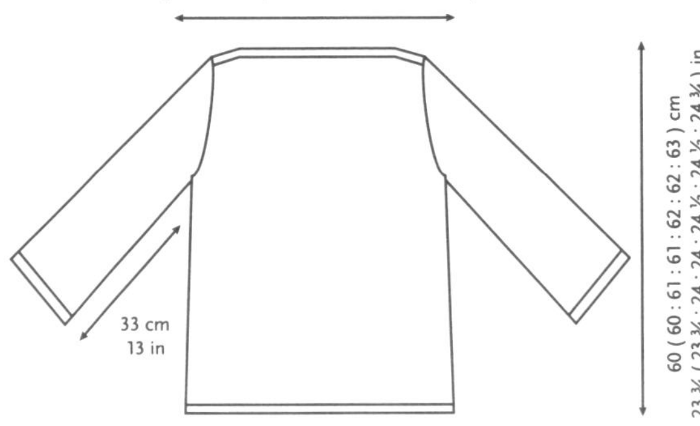

BACK AND FRONT (both alike)

With 3mm (US 2) circular needle and M cast on 105(113:121:129:137:145:153) sts.
K 7(7:9:9:11:11:13) rows.
Change to 3.25mm (US 3) circular needle.
Beg with a k row work in st st and stripes of 12 rows C and 14 rows M throughout.
Work 132(130:130:128:128:126:126) rows, ending 2(14:14:12:12:10:10) rows C(M:M:M:M:M:M).

Shape armholes

Cast off 4(5:5:6:6:7:7) sts at beg of next 2 rows.
97(103:111:117:125:131:139) sts.
Next row K3, skpo, k to last 5 sts, k2 tog, k3.
Next row P to end.
Rep the last 2 rows 2(2:3:3:4:4:5) times more.
91(97:103:109:115:121:127) sts.
Work 54(56:54:56:54:56:54) rows straight, ending 12 rows C.
Change to 3mm (US 2) needles and M.
K 7(7:9:9:11:11:13) rows.

Shoulders

K14(16:18:20:22:24:26) sts, leave these sts on a holder, cast off next 63(65:67:69:71:73:75) sts, k to end, leave these 14(16:18:20:22:24:26) sts on a holder.

SLEEVES

With 3mm (US 2) needles and M cast on 70(74:78:82:86:90:94) sts.
K 7(7:9:9:11:11:13) rows.
Change to 3.25mm (US 3) needles.
Beg with a k row work in st st and stripes of 12 rows C and 14 rows M throughout.
Work 106(104:104:102:102:100:100) rows, ending 2(14:14:12:12:10:10) rows C(M:M:M:M:M:M).

Shape top

Cast off 4(5:5:6:6:7:7) sts at beg of next 2 rows.
62(64:68:70:74:76:80) sts.
Next row K1, skpo, k to last 3 sts, k2 tog, k1.
Next row P to end.
Rep the last 2 rows 10(10:11:11:12:12:13) times more.
40(42:44:46:48:50:52) sts.
Next row K1, skpo, k to last 3 sts, k2 tog, k1.
Work 3 rows.
Rep the last 4 rows 3 times more.
32(34:36:38:40:42:44) sts.
Next row K1, skpo, k to last 3 sts, k2 tog, k1.
Next row P to end.
Rep the last 2 rows once more.
28(30:32:34:36:38:40) sts.
Cast off 3 sts at beg of next 4 rows.
Cast off.

MAKE UP

Join shoulders by placing sts on holders with wrong sides together and knitting one st together from front and back and casting them off on right side.
Join side and sleeve seams. Sew in sleeves.

YARN COLOURS

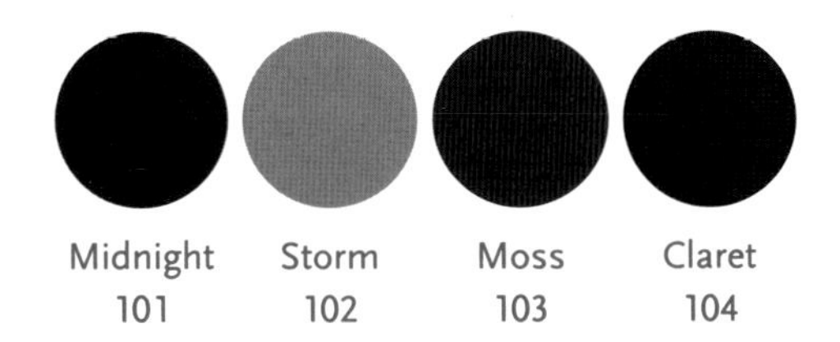

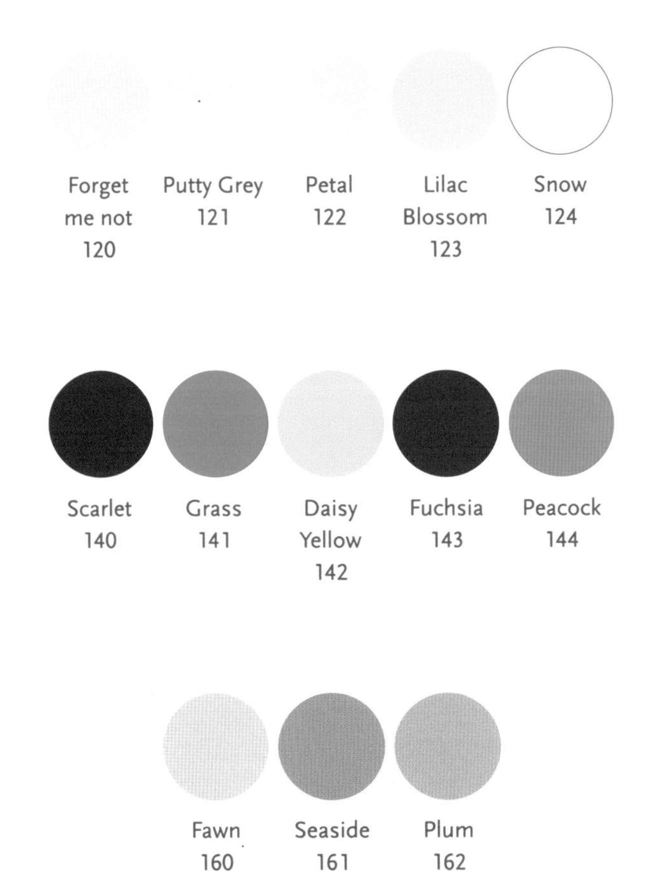

INDEX

FROM MILLAMIA

We are finally here! Launching our first MillaMia collection of knitting patterns for adults. We are excited, scared, proud, hopeful – it really does feel like a turning point for us. For those who know our brand from before, you will be familiar with the high standards we have tried to achieve with our babies and children's knitting patterns using our Naturally Soft Merino yarn range. With four well-received books to date we naturally had some apprehension when embarking on this project. Could we hope to measure up to our kids' products?

We knew we had to try. One of the constants since we launched with 'The Close Knit Gang' in 2009, has been repeated customer requests for us to create our designs as adult patterns. These requests became more frequent with each collection we published and in the end they were impossible to ignore.

Helena had the challenge of looking through our catalogue of designs to date, and deciding which patterns would be appropriate to adapt, more or less as-is, to adult versions. We have literally taken you – our customers – and your feedback at face value.

You said you wanted the Charlotte Cardigan from Wonderland for adults, now you have it. Adapted of course to fit a grown up female shape and size, but more or less the same item – renamed the Charlie Cardigan. Ditto the Stefan Jacket for the men. Any of you planning to knit matching father and son Stefan and Alexander Jackets? (See Wonderland pattern book for the boy's version).

Other patterns are hybrid items – taking elements of our most popular styles but adapting them to make them more wearable or knittable. Still more are brand new, coming from Helena's recent inspiration.

Again for those familiar with our previous work it might be fun to see how well the patterns do indeed translate to adult garments. In some cases we have made slightly different colour choices with an adult wearer in mind and this has been part of the fun of the process. It has been fantastic to see how well the yarn has adapted to this other usage. We already knew it was great for children's patterns and interior products, now we know that adult hand knitters can also benefit from its softness, great stitch definition and rewarding colour palette.

We hope you enjoy this book, and our designs. We have another two adult collections already in the pipeline which we cannot wait to share with you. We'll be sure to tell you a bit more about the process in each book – perhaps the next instalment will focus on how we chose our male models? Finally for those who love our children's patterns – don't worry we won't neglect new patterns for this audience too. Katarina has not just the adult collections in the pipeline but also a new baby, so expect perhaps a focus on smaller items in the next year too!

With best wishes,
Katarina and Helena Rosén
katarina@millamia.com or helena@millamia.com